# HARRY'S ABORTION

## by

## D. J. Connolly

## April, 2011

# INTRODUCTION

Perhaps you saw the 1968 movie, *2001, A Space Odyssey*. Even if you aren't old enough to have seen it in 1968, it's probably still available on videotape or DVD. The movie, a science fiction classic, had three parts, perhaps the most interesting being the middle part that described the beginning of a manned mission to Jupiter. Such a bold mission might seem ridiculous now; but in 1968 it seemed like a reasonable extension of the remarkable progress America's space program was then making.

The spacecraft was controlled by several astronauts and Hal 9000, a very smart computer. Scientists had created Hal to help and serve the crew. In response to a question from a BBC reporter, Hal boasted that he (it) was practically "foolproof and incapable of error."

As I recall, the planned Jupiter mission required eighteen months for completion. After a few weeks a fairly serious fault turned up in one of Hal's logic modules; and a profound difference of opinion arose over how best to diagnose and repair it. The human crew favored one approach and Hal favored another. Since he (it) was "incapable of error," Hal thought it best that he take complete control; and he (it) began murdering the astronauts by cutting off their life support systems.

One-hundred years after "We the People" ratified the 14th Amendment, which the Supreme Court perverted five years later to protect and promote abortion, the movie depicted Hal aborting his human masters. In the first abortion Hal used a robotic claw-arm to cut the air hose of Frank, an astronaut working outside the vehicle. He (it) used similar means to abort the others.

1

Hal managed to abort all the human crewmen except one. Dave Bowman survived long enough to pull the plug connecting Hal to his power supply. Dave subsequently piloted the spacecraft to Jupiter unassisted; but he didn't get back home. If you want to find out how the movie ends shop around for a copy.

"We the People" created a judicial branch of government to decide "cases and controversies" under our laws and our Constitution. But it, like Hal, has gone berserk. Instead of obeying our laws and our Constitution it makes up its own laws and its own constitution and imposes them on us. Like Hal 9000 aborting its human masters, our judicial branch of government is aborting our children. It's probably not reasonable to blame the Supreme Court for all fifty million (and growing) abortions since *Roe v. Wade* (1973); perhaps as many as half would have occurred without that infamous act. Nevertheless, 25 million (and growing) killings puts our judicial branch of government in the same class as Hitler's Germany and Stalin's USSR.

This little monograph was excerpted from a much longer book, **Grand Larceny: An Unexpurgated History of the Supreme Court**. I focused **Harry's Abortion** on the most scandalous fraud perpetrated by America's judicial branch of government during the 20th century, its rulings on abortion. The first chapter summarizes *Roe v. Wade* (1973) and the historical facts that prove it's as bogus as a three dollar bill. Roe was followed a few years later by *Planned Parenthood v. Casey* (1992) and *Stenberg v. Carhart* (2000). Chapter 2 describes these two rulings and the historical facts that prove they're also fraudulent.

Chapters 3 and 4 describe the birth and development of the "due process scam," the lawyers' con job the Court used to justify these three bogus rulings.

America's political, journalistic, and academic elites do not want the public to learn that the U. S. Supreme Court is a criminal enterprise. And various political factions do not want you to learn that *Roe* and the other abortion rulings are fraudulent. So professors, journalists, and politicians have busied themselves, over the years, making up cover stories to convince you that our judiciary is on the up and up. Chapters 5 and 6 discuss and dissect those cover stories.

The abortion rulings cannot be understood apart from the fact that the Court has long been running a pagan anti-Christian religion in violation of the First Amendment. Chapter 7 exposes and explores that dirty little secret [1].

### INTRODUCTION END NOTES

1. Every Supreme Court opinion mentioned in this monograph can be found on the Internet using a commercial search engine. I do not quote Internet addresses for Supreme Court opinions because the addresses tend to change from time to time.

# CHAPTER 1: THE GANG OF SEVEN

In 1968 we elected Richard Nixon President of the United States. He had run on a platform that included a promise to reform the federal courts. Nixon said he would appoint judges who would "strictly construe" the Constitution rather than stealth legislators who would usurp the power to amend it. Somehow it didn't work out as he had promised. Nixon gave us the Burger Court that sat from 1969 through 1986. The Burger Court manufactured bogus constitutional amendments like jellybeans.

Its most famous bogus amendment came in 1973. That year the Court handed down *Roe v. Wade*, a piece of fiction that nullified the abortion laws of forty-nine states, nineteen of which had recently liberalized those laws. Public opinion was becoming more tolerant of abortion and the states were changing their laws to reflect that trend. Ignoring our constitutional guarantee of a "Republican Form of Government," our judicial employees snatched control of the abortion issue away from "We the People" anyway.

Three out of four Nixon appointees were among the Gang of Seven that voted for the majority opinion. Chief Justice Warren Burger, who Nixon chose to lead the Court away from Earl Warren's buccaneer ways, voted for it. Harry Blackmun, Nixon's second nominee, wrote it. Only William Rehnquist and Byron White, a Kennedy appointee, voted no.

White expressed concern about the Court's image. It was planning to gut all America's capital punishment laws around the same time it decided *Roe v. Wade*. Taken together, those two rulings would send an awful message about the Court's values. It would seem to prefer killing the innocent rather than the guilty. Some of the more liberal justices just smiled. The Second Great Commandment of Acluism demands that we punish the innocent and reward the guilty [1].

Millions of Americans now cling to *Roe v. Wade*, a judicial invention they believe is somehow based on the Constitution. The ruling, however, had no basis in the Constitution; and the Gang of Seven made only a half-hearted effort to hide that fact. Legal scholars, therefore, reacted with distaste [2].

Legal scholars are not surprised when the Supreme Court 'evolves' the Constitution. But they expect a convincing cover story. A clumsy evolution risks loss of public trust in our "rule of law." Even the Court's young law clerks saw Blackmun's opinion for the pathetic piece of fiction that it was; they called it "Harry's Abortion." As a constitutional interpretation they thought it was absurd. They were also embarrassed by the plain fact that it had resulted from political horse trading among the justices rather than judicial loyalty to any constitutional principle [3].

## DUE PROCESS MISCHIEF

The Gang of Seven had decided to find a right to abortion in the Constitution. And they needed a credible story to explain how and when that right got there. This was a bit of a challenge since the Constitution mentions neither a right to abortion nor a generalized right to "privacy." So they asserted that the founders empowered them to include these things at the proper time. However, the historical evidence proved exactly the opposite. Our founders thought abortion was an abomination. It was illegal when all the relevant constitutional passages were

6

adopted.

In 1791, when America adopted the Bill of Rights, the common law, which was followed in every state, prohibited abortion after "quickening" (the mother's first perception of fetal life within her, usually at about 17 weeks of pregnancy). Harry Blackmun's majority opinion acknowledged this fact. Blackmun disposed of this objection with a long, inane discussion, the central point of which was that abortion after "quickening" was probably not a felony, but only a misdemeanor.

Right! Our founders must have intended to protect abortion in the Bill of Rights, along with freedom of religion and freedom of speech, because they didn't make it a felony, only a misdemeanor. No doubt that bit of humbug was part of the reason the clerks called Blackmun's opinion "Harry's Abortion." In any case, the Gang of Seven relied mainly on the 14th Amendment rather than the Bill of Rights. After about 8000 words of sophistry, they got to the bottom line [4].

> "A state criminal abortion statute of the current Texas type, that excepts from criminality only a lifesaving procedure on behalf of the mother, without regard to pregnancy stage and without recognition of the other interests involved, is violative of the Due Process Clause of the Fourteenth Amendment."

Let's submit that claim to a little sanity test. The 14th Amendment was ratified by the necessary three-fourths (28 out of 37) of the states by July 9, 1868. Twenty-three of the twenty-eight ratifying states had anti-abortion laws on the books when they ratified it. And many of them treated abortion as a felony not a misdemeanor.

You will not be surprised to learn that nobody, at the

time the Amendment was ratified, mentioned the possibility that it might nullify all those laws, many of which had been passed in the prior few years. The Gang of Seven would have us believe that our forefathers ratified the 14th Amendment, realizing it might nullify laws they had just passed, and nobody mentioned that possibility. Everybody on the Court was aware of this history; Justice Rehnquist summarized it in his dissenting opinion. No doubt that's also part of reason the clerks called Blackmun's opinion "Harry's Abortion" [5].

Actually, the historical evidence condemned the majority opinion even more emphatically than Rehnquist's dissent had suggested. The states passed a blizzard of new anti abortion laws about the same time they ratified the 14th Amendment. Many of those laws specifically excepted "from criminality only a lifesaving (abortion) procedure on behalf of the mother, without regard to pregnancy stage and without recognition of the other interests involved." Many of those laws also passed by overwhelming majorities [6].

The Ohio Legislature toughened the State's anti abortion laws in 1867, the same year it ratified the 14th Amendment. It voted in April 1867 to make abortion illegal at any stage of pregnancy. The Senate vote was 21-8, the House vote, 53-30. Later in 1867 the same Ohio Senate that ratified the 14th Amendment voted unanimously to outlaw "the publication, sale, or gratuitous distribution of drugs, medicines, and nostrums intended to prevent conception, or procure abortion."

Illinois also toughened its anti-abortion laws in 1867, the same year it voted to ratify the 14th Amendment, raising the penalty for performing an abortion to at least two and not more than ten years. The bill passed unanimously in both Houses [6].

8

Florida ratified the 14th Amendment on June 9, 1868. During the same session, it revised its abortion laws to outlaw any attempted abortion at any stage of gestation. The penalty was set at one to seven years in prison. The Florida statute and the Ohio statute (mentioned above) were virtually unchanged in 1973 when the Gang of Seven opined that their authors, in voting to ratify the 14th Amendment, had intended to make their own contemporaneous legislative work "violative of the Due Process Clause" of that same Amendment [7].

Both Vermont and New York passed tough new anti-abortion legislation in the year following their ratification of the 14th Amendment. The 1867 Vermont law outlawed abortion at any stage of the pregnancy and outlawed the "advertisement and distribution of abortificant materials or information." The 1868 New York law outlawed the advertising of abortion (and contraceptives). New York followed up in 1869 with legislation to criminalize abortion at any stage of the pregnancy. New York toughened its abortion laws twice more within the next few years [8].

Within a fifteen-year period (1860-1875) centered about the ratification of the 14th Amendment, 16 of the 28 ratifying states toughened their anti-abortion laws. Most of that legislation criminalized abortion "without regard to pregnancy stage and without recognition of the other interests involved." Much of it also excepted "from criminality only a lifesaving procedure on behalf of the mother." Congress tacitly endorsed this legislative trend by passing the so-called Comstock Law in 1873 [9].

The above information was readily available to the Gang of Seven when they all voted for "Harry's Abortion." It was also available to the various justices who voted, during the past 30 years, to uphold this outrageous fraud. Put aside, for a moment, your personal view as to whether or to what extent the laws ought to restrict abortion; and consider a more urgent question. Do you want your judicial employees trashing the Constitution and imposing their preferred abortion policies by royal decree? Do you want your judicial employees trashing your Constitution for any cause [10]?

## CHAPTER 1 END NOTES

1. The two Great Commandments of Acluism, are described in Chapter 7. Justice White's concern for the Court's image is described in McKeever, pages 56-7.

2. Glendon cited six prominent legal scholars who criticized *Roe v. Wade.* See her pages 44, 171, and 172. McKeever's Chapter 4 also contains an account of the adverse reaction of legal scholars to the opinion.

3. A discussion of the legal fiction that our Constitution "evolves" can be found in Chapter 6. A description of the Supreme Court clerks' reaction to "Harry's Abortion" can be found in Woodward, page 276. The opinion relied heavily on *Griswold v. Connecticut* which announced that the Constitution contains "penumbras" which, from time to time, "emanate" startling new judicial powers.

4. The passage quoted here is from Justice Blackmun's majority opinion in *Roe v. Wade.*

5. Dates of state legislation to ratify the 14th Amendment can be found in a table opposite page 214 in Fairman and Morrison. Dates of anti-abortion legislation contemporaneous with the drafting and ratification of the 14th Amendment can be found in the book by Mohr. See also Justice Rehnquist's dissenting opinion in *Roe v. Wade.*

6. See Mohr, Chapter Seven.

7. See Mohr, Chapter Seven. See also the Roe majority opinion.

8. Vermont ratified the Constitution in 1866 and New York in 1867. Vermont passed anti-abortion legislation in 1867 and New York in 1868, 1869, 1872, and 1875. See Mohr, pages 210-219.

9. The sixteen states were Connecticut (1860), Illinois, Ohio, and Vermont (1867), Florida and New York (1868), Michigan, Massachusetts, and Nevada (1869), Louisiana and Pennsylvania (1870), New Jersey (1872), Minnesota and Nebraska (1873), Kansas (1874), and Arkansas (1875). The foregoing list is not all-inclusive; some of these states toughened their anti-abortion laws more than once during the period in question. To review the content of these laws see Mohr, Chapter Seven. The federal Comstock Act of 1873 made it a felony to publish, distribute, or possess "information about or devices or medications for unlawful abortion or contraception." The maximum penalty was five years at hard labor plus a $2000 fine.

10. The folks who ratified the 14th Amendment would have been outraged at the idea that the Supreme Court, which they then viewed with contempt, would have the gall to fabricate fraudulent new content in their brand new Amendment. They viewed the Amendment's main purpose as nullifying the Dred Scott Decision, an earlier Supreme Court fraud. See Chapter 3.

# CHAPTER 2: OBSTRUCTION OF JUSTICE

Imagine, for a moment, that you have a sister named Gwendolyn. Gwen has lousy taste in men; lately she's been hanging around with a reputed drug lord named Dudley. The police are convinced that Dudley recently shot and killed a rival dope dealer. You've just learned that Gwendolyn lied to the police to give Dudley an alibi. She said they were both having dinner at your home during the evening of the murder. Now the cops are coming around to question you. What are you going to do? If you don't back up your sister, she'll be charged with obstruction of justice. If you do, you might be charged too.

Supreme Court justices often confront a similar choice. When that happens, they usually choose to obstruct justice. Only they made up a Latin name for their crime to conceal the fact that it's a crime; they call it the rule of stare decisis. That means they won't overturn an earlier Supreme Court precedent, even one that's clearly fraudulent. The Mafia used to call it the rule of omerta.

## THE ADJUDICATION OF SUBSTANTIVE DUE PROCESS CLAIMS

In 1992 the Supreme Court decided *Planned Parenthood v. Casey*. This case, which involved various state rules concerning abortion clinics, was a perfect opportunity to dump the *Roe v. Wade* precedent. A majority of the justices reportedly had admitted privately that it was based on fiction. Yet part of that majority voted to follow the rule of omerta and retain it. Three "centrists" (as characterized by various press reports) wrote an opinion stating in part,

> "After considering the fundamental constitutional questions resolved by *Roe*, principles of institutional integrity, and the rule of stare decisis, we are led to conclude this: the essential holding of *Roe v. Wade* should be retained and once again reaffirmed."

The three "centrists" went on to say,

> "Constitutional protection of the woman's decision to terminate her pregnancy derives from the Due Process Clause of the Fourteenth Amendment. It declares that no State shall "deprive any person of life, liberty, or property, without due process of law." The controlling word in the case before us is "liberty." Although a literal reading of the Clause might suggest that it governs only the procedures by which a State may deprive persons of liberty, for at least 105 years, at least since *Mugler v. Kansas*, (1887), the Clause has been understood to contain a substantive component as well, one barring certain government actions regardless of the fairness of the procedures used to implement them."

We'll come back to *Mugler v. Kansas* in a minute. But first it's important to point out that this was not the first case in which the Supreme Court asserted that the clause "due process of law" has a "substantive component." The "three centrists" would not dare to admit that the court's invention of a "substantive component" in the "due process clause" originated in the Dred Scott opinion, a Supreme Court opinion even they would admit smells to high Heaven. We'll discuss that subject in Chapter 3.

Now let's get back to *Mugler v. Kansas*. In 1887 a band of judicial buccaneers on the Waite Court declared that the authors of the 14th Amendment intended it to protect

14

bootleggers from the laws and constitution of the State of Kansas. In 1883, that same band of renegades had reached the startling conclusion that the 14th Amendment did not empower Congress to pass a law securing the right of African Americans to enjoy equal access to inns, railroads, and other public accommodations. They went on, in 1887, to assert it was perfectly obvious that corporations were "persons" entitled to the protection of the 14th Amendment. The Fourteenth Amendment begins: "All persons born or naturalized in the United States." Does that support the claim that our founders intended the Fourteenth Amendment to protect corporations from regulation by the states in which they operated [1]?

The infamous Waite Court subverted the 14th Amendment from its intended purpose, to protect the rights of recently freed slaves, and fashioned it into a general-purpose tool for judges to use to usurp control of state laws. Most of its members should have been hung. Consequently, the three "centrists" (their names were O'Connor, Kennedy, and Souter) reached defective conclusions about the "fundamental constitutional questions" they 'considered.' And "stare decisis" is just a variation on the Mafia code of silence. So all they had left to justify their actions were "principles of institutional integrity." The three "centrists" have a strange definition of "integrity."

## A SLIPPERY SLOPE

You probably already know all you care to about "partial birth abortion." The Supreme Court (quoting the State of Nebraska) has defined it as "a procedure in which the doctor partially delivers vaginally a living unborn child before killing the . . . child." The Court went on to

15

assert, in *Stenberg v. Carhart* (2000), that "Nebraska's statute criminalizing the performance of "partial birth abortion[s]" violates the Federal Constitution, as interpreted in *Casey and Roe.*" Rule 2 has led the Court down a very slippery slope. It has now admitted that the logic of *Roe* and *Casey* leads inexorably to the grotesque claim that the Constitution safeguards the right of "killing the . . . child" [2].

**CHAPTER 2 END NOTES**
1. For an account of the two other bogus Waite Court opinions mentioned above (besides *Mugler v. Kansas)*, see Chapters 12 and 13 in Connolly, 2010.

2. The three "centrists" used the words "kill" or "killing" five times to describe procedures they alleged the Constitution protects.

# CHAPTER 3: A SCAM IS BORN

Every few seconds someone gets a phone call from a place the cops call a "boiler room." There's no boiler there, just desks and telephones. Con artists are using the telephones to call up folks looking for victims. When they find one, they try to sell her a thousand shares of phony stock or five acres in the middle of a swamp. The con artists need to make a lot of calls because they usually have a very low hit rate. Most of their targets refuse to listen to their pitch much less be victimized.

There's another confidence racket that's much more sophisticated than the average boiler room pitch. Hustlers have long worked this racket in courtrooms all over America. And it's had a very big impact on all our lives. Lawyers call it the "substantive due process doctrine." In this book we're simply going to call it the "due process scam." The due process scam is a big, nasty mutant. The Supreme Court "evolved" it just before the Civil War. In fact, one could make a case that it caused the Civil War. It has continued to grow bigger and nastier ever since. And it's still devouring your rights.

In 1857 the Supreme Court decided the case of *Dred Scott v. Sandford*. The Chief Justice at the time was a fellow named Roger Taney. The Taney Court did what the Supreme Court often does. It first picked the outcome it wanted then found a few scraps of evidence to support that outcome, ignoring or distorting a much larger volume of evidence to the contrary. It then issued a decision claiming that its desired outcome was demanded by the Constitution.

History books say the main issue in the Dred Scott case was the power of Congress, under the Constitution, to restrict slavery in the territories. Most of the founders viewed slavery as morally repugnant. And they thought it would die out, given enough time. They relied on political give and take to end it in a peaceful way [1].

As part of the give and take, Congress had enacted the Missouri Compromise in 1820. Among other things it forbade slavery in the Wisconsin Territory. Dred Scott was an elderly slave who sued Mr. Sandford, his owner, for his freedom. A former master had taken Scott into the Wisconsin Territory, stayed there for a while, and then brought him back to Missouri, a state that permitted slavery. Mr. Scott's lawyer claimed that living in Wisconsin had made him free by virtue of the Missouri Compromise.

Mr. Sandford's lawyer needed a way to deal with that claim. So he asked the Court to suddenly discover that the thirty-seven-year-old Missouri Compromise was unconstitutional. The Court went along with that. The record shows that Roger Taney and the other judges who voted with him were hopelessly biased in favor of Southern slave owners.

At that time it looked like slavery's days were numbered. Public opinion against it in the North was growing. And the North was gaining people and wealth faster than the South. The justices were looking for a way to put their thumbs on the scale of justice and tip the political balance back in favor of the slave owners. In searching for a pretext to justify what they wanted to do, they focused on the idea of slaves as property. The Fifth Amendment said that nobody could be deprived of "life, liberty, or property, without due process of law." The Court said that the Constitution hadn't spelled out in so many words that Congress had a right to control "property" in the U. S.

18

territories. Therefore, the Missouri Compromise lacked a foundation in "due process of law." So it violated the Fifth Amendment.

This ruling was a big surprise to most well informed Americans at the time. They knew that the Constitution said, "Congress shall have power to dispose of and make all needful Rules and Regulations respecting the Territory or other Property belonging to the United States" [2].

They also knew about the Northwest Ordinance, first enacted by the Continental Congress in 1787. The Northwest Ordinance laid down rules for the governing of a large territory northwest of the Ohio River, land that subsequently became five states. Among other things, the Ordinance provided that:

> "There shall be neither slavery nor involuntary servitude in the said territory, otherwise than in the punishment of crimes, whereof the party shall have been duly convicted: Provided always, that any person escaping into the same, from whom labor or service is lawfully claimed in any one of the original States, such fugitive may be lawfully reclaimed, and conveyed to the person claiming his or her labor or service as aforesaid" [2].

During the same year that representatives of the thirteen original states wrote the above language, other representatives (in some cases the same men) wrote our new Constitution in Philadelphia. It was ratified by the states and took effect the following year. And the Continental Congress went out of business to make way for the new U. S. Congress, which promptly reaffirmed the Northwest Ordinance in 1789. That was the same year it proposed the Fifth Amendment to the states for ratification.

Informed Americans in 1857, therefore, thought it

obvious that the Missouri Compromise couldn't possibly be unconstitutional. It had basically the same effect on "property" in the territories as did the Northwest Ordinance which representatives of "We the People" had passed and then reaffirmed at essentially the same time they ratified the Constitution. So the Dred Scott decision was clearly a fraud.

Informed Americans also knew that the founders intended the term "due process" to control the acts of judges, not legislators. The great constitutional authority, Alexander Hamilton, had said, on the record,

> "The words due process have a precise technical import, and are only applicable to the process and proceedings of the courts of justice, they can never be referred to an act of the legislature."

Legislatures had control over the substance of laws and courts controlled only the processes by which the laws were applied to individual cases. Nobody ever accused Hamilton of being biased against broad powers for judges. He liked broad powers for judges. He was biased against any real power for the people. The intended meaning of "due process," therefore, was completely settled among our founders [3].

The justices on the Taney Court had thought their deception was fairly safe. The common people had a lot of respect for the Supreme Court. They didn't know much history. And they didn't have a clue what "due process" was supposed to mean. All they knew was that it sounded important. So the Court just made up a new meaning. However, Republican newspapers explained what a fraud the Dred Scott ruling was. They also exposed the fact that the judges were biased. Abraham Lincoln and others charged that members of the Supreme Court were working a plot to force slavery on the entire nation [4].

In a speech in Cincinnati, Ohio in September of 1859, Lincoln suggested what should be done about a renegade Supreme Court.

> "The people of these United States are the rightful masters of both congresses and courts, not to overthrow the Constitution, but to overthrow the men who would pervert the Constitution" [5].

The people responded by electing, in 1860, Abe Lincoln and others who had promised to "overthrow the men who would pervert the Constitution". Southern slave owners saw political defeat staring them in the face. So they went to war to obtain the justice that the Court had said was theirs. To that end they took on a much larger and richer power. The North had more than twice the Southern (free) population and six times the Southern manufacturing capacity. It had far superior naval strength and manufactured almost all the nation's firearms. Only in agriculture, morale, and in the quality of their military officers could the Southern States compete. Their morale and the quality of their officers kept them in the game for a while. But they lacked resources and they lacked bench strength. The Northern States were guaranteed to win, given a little time. For the South, the Civil War was insane [6].

The majority of white Southerners didn't own any slaves and had nothing to gain from the war. In fact, the institution of slavery was quite damaging to their interests. How does one compete in the labor market against four million people who work for room and board? But poor Southerners were conned by their wealthier neighbors into believing that the Constitution was on their side. Truth and justice were on their side. The high priests of the Supreme

Court had told them so. Fraudulent action by those high priests led to a Civil War that caused a million casualties [7].

We were taught in school that the Civil War resolved the issue of slavery. We learned that the Dred Scott case was a milestone in the sequence of events that led to the war. We also learned that history judged the decision to be wrong. However, our teachers never told us that a bogus Supreme Court decision caused the Civil War. That would be in poor taste. You are not supposed to learn that a fraudulent Supreme Court decision caused a million casualties. Modern writers occasionally hint that it did. But the idea is not popular among journalists, politicians, and educators. They prefer that you keep your illusions about our judiciary [8].

Northern Americans in the Civil War era had no such illusions. In 1861 The New York Tribune wrote,

> "The present rebellion ... is due quite as much to an unsound and unwise decision of the Supreme Court as to any other single cause" [9].

During an 1865 debate in Congress, Massachusetts Senator Charles Sumner said that the

> "wicked opinion of (Chief Justice Taney)" in the Dred Scott case was the "incident of our history," prior to the Civil War, "most deadly in its consequences" [10].

During the same debate, Senator Henry Wilson, also of Massachusetts, said that Taney had done more to plunge the nation into "this bloody revolution" than any other person, and that the Dred Scott decision was "the greatest crime in the judicial annals of the Republic" [10].

Three years later "We the People" adopted the 14th Amendment, in part to consign the Dred Scott opinion to the junk bin of history. But the due process scam, the monster to which the opinion gave birth, lives on. It claims new victims every year.

## CHAPTER 3 END NOTES

1. See D'Souza, 1995, for a discussion of the founders' attitudes toward slavery. The Dred Scott ruling is described in many places. See, for example, Berger, Swisher, Fairman (1970), and Fehrenbacher.

2. The Constitutional language quoted is in Article IV, Section 3. The text of the Northwest Ordinance can be found online using a commercial search engine.

3. The Alexander Hamilton quote can be found in Berger, 1977, page 196. Hamilton was speaking to the New York Assembly in February 1787. For other comments on the historical meaning of "due process," see Black, 1968, Chapter II, Berger, 1977, pages 193-200, or Rodell, 1957, pages 56-58. Hamilton's mistrust of "the people" is well documented. He reportedly said, in a debate with Thomas Jefferson, "the people, sir, is nothing but a great beast." See Platt, page 251.

4. See Fehrenbacher, Chapters 21-23, for an account of the history of the Dred Scott decision. The bias of the Taney Court majority is described in Swisher, Chapters 23 and 24; Berger, 1977, pages 222-3; and McCloskey, pages 59-66. See also Heckman, pages 74 and 85.

5. Lincoln is quoted by Senator Jenner during the August 20, 1958 debates on the Jenner- Butler Bill. See the 1958 Congressional Record Senate, page 18645.

6. See Phillips, page 384.

7. See, for example, Abbott page 4. Casualty statistics were taken from Price, 1961. The use of the term "high priests" to describe the members of the Court is explained

in Chapter 7.

8.  The notion that the Dred Scott decision helped cause the Civil War is mentioned in a few modern sources.  See, for example, Bork, 1990, Fehrenbacher, 1978, and especially, Acheson, 1961.  Fehrenbacher (page 573) has a quote from Acheson (page 120) saying that the Dred Scott decision "practically started a war."  I have not seen the point made any stronger than that.

9.  See Silver, page 47.

10.  See Silver, pages 225-6.  See also Warren (Charles, Vol. 3) page 117.

# CHAPTER 4: EVOLUTION OF A SCAM

Perhaps you are among those who believe that punishment does not deter crime or, what's essentially the same thing, most men and women will obey the law in the absence of fear of punishment. If you believe that, look around while driving on the Interstate and see if most drivers appear to be observing the speed limit. Better yet, look at your own speedometer. Most of us will not obey a law unless we expect it to be enforced.

In 1804 the House of Representatives impeached a Supreme Court justice named Samuel Chase. Chase had been the loudest and most obnoxious of a group of justices who trashed the Bill of Rights [1].

Unfortunately, the impeachment failed in the Senate; the vote to convict fell short of the constitutionally required two-thirds majority. The Federalists in the Senate voted as a bloc to protect Chase; and several Republicans declined to support removal of a Supreme Court justice for what some might consider political reasons. They thought it would set a bad precedent [1].

A worse, even disastrous, precedent was set as a result of the failure. Future Supreme Court justices took the lesson that it was virtually impossible to keep them honest. If Justice Chase couldn't be fired for openly trashing the Constitution in service of a partisan political agenda, they (the justices) could evidently get away with any political crime they chose to perpetrate. All they needed was a credible cover story.

## A CREDIBLE COVER STORY

If you've already read Chapter 3, you know that a fraudulent U. S. Supreme Court ruling led to the Civil War. You also know that it gave birth to the due process scam, the most successful con game in American history. This Chapter will follow the subsequent development of the scam [2].

The due process scam, as invented in the Dred Scott case, was based on a perversion of the 'due process clause' of the Fifth Amendment, which says that, no person shall "be deprived of life, liberty, or property, without due process of law." There can be no honest doubt about the intended meaning of the phrase, "due process of law." It was universally understood, by our founders to apply only to trials. It meant a fair trial which followed traditional procedures including conviction by a jury of one's peers. Our founders trusted ordinary citizens a lot more than they trusted judges. And they wanted to insure that no judge could punish anybody without first going through a "process" in which ordinary citizens were empowered to keep him honest. As noted in chapter 3, the constitutional author and explicator, Alexander Hamilton, said in 1787,

> "The words due process have a precise technical import, and are only applicable to the process and proceedings of the courts of justice. They can never be referred to an act of the legislature."

With the possible exception of James Madison, Hamilton was the foremost expounder, among its framers, of the intended meaning of the Constitution. He was also a strong supporter of broad powers for courts and, among our founders, had an uncommonly low degree of trust for legislatures accountable to "the people." The fact that he, above all others, made the foregoing statement shows that it represented the virtually unanimous understanding of our founders [3].

There also can be no honest doubt about the intended meaning of the phrase, "deprived of life, liberty, or property." It referred to punishment for crimes. In our founders' society, the death penalty was administered for a variety of crimes including murder, rape, sodomy, and, in two states, even blasphemy. "Deprived of liberty" meant thrown into jail and "deprived of property" meant having one's property taken as punishment for a crime [4].

The foregoing describes everything our founders intended the "due process clause" of the Fifth Amendment to mean. In 1857, a renegade Supreme Court invented a completely new meaning for the clause and used it to nullify a law passed by Congress, a law whose only defect was that a majority of the justices found it distasteful. That bit of judicial mischief, the Dred Scott Decision, led to the Civil War.

After the Civil War ended, Congress finally got around to responding to the Court's brazen power grab. It proposed the 14th Amendment. The Amendment contained language intended to nullify the Dred Scott decision. And it declared that Congress, rather that the courts, would have power to enforce it.

However, Congress shot itself in the foot. It didn't make sufficient allowance for the gall of future Supreme Court justices. It used the same "due process" language in the first paragraph of the 14th Amendment that the Court had perverted (as Abe Lincoln said) to justify the Dred Scott decision [5].

Contemporaneous with the framing and ratification of the Amendment, Congress passed four "enforcement acts" as the Amendment explicitly authorized. The four acts, which ran in total to over 8000 words, contained everything that Congress intended the 14th Amendment to cover. They were completely devoid of any support for a broad new construction of the "due process" clause. One can confirm that statement by going to Appendix B of Connolly, 2010, and reviewing the four acts.

After laying low for a few years, the Supreme Court, under various pretexts, nullified the four enforcement acts, thereby protecting three-quarters-of-a-century of Ku Klux Klan outrages and Jim Crow laws in much of the South [6].

That is not to say that the Supreme Court nullified the 14th Amendment. Instead the Court broadened the due process scam to subvert the Amendment to its own corrupt purposes. The Court used, and still uses, fraudulent interpretations of the Fifth and 14th Amendments to nullify the first sentence in the U. S. Constitution [7].

## LIFE, LIBERTY, AND PROPERTY

If you torture the plain meaning of words without conscience, you can come up with a story line to justify almost anything. In evolving the due process scam, the justices decided to see how far they could stretch the words, "liberty" and "property" as used in the Fifth and 14th Amendments. With a sufficiently broad definition of those two words, there's no law that Congress or a state legislature might enact that could not be alleged to infringe on somebody's "rights" under the substantive due process doctrine.

A tax obviously takes somebody's property. So the doctrine gives courts, rather than Congress, the final say on the reasonableness of any tax. A law forbidding predatory or fraudulent behavior by corporations can be attacked as depriving some company of the most advantageous use of

28

its "property." The Court might not strike down the law; but then again it might. It depends on whether or not the justices like the law, not on any real constitutional issue.

Even an appropriation of public funds is fair game for due process mischief. A plaintiff who did not get a government handout he expected can claim he had a "property right" to the handout and petition a court to review the appropriation for conformance with some judge-made rule regarding "due process."

The possibilities for substantive due process mischief based on the word "liberty" boggle the mind. A law against murder, rape, burglary, or dope peddling tends to restrict the "liberty" of murderers, rapists, burglars, and dope peddlers. The Supreme Court has not yet supported a claim that this type of law denies "due process;" but it's not really all that far-fetched to predict it some day will. Our Founders would have been aghast at the idea that federal courts might some day construe the Fifth or 14th Amendment to protect homosexual sodomy or abortion. But that's exactly what they did.

To be sure, "We the People" don't feel the same way about the issues of homosexual sodomy and abortion we did when we ratified the relevant Amendments. However, we're perfectly capable of changing our laws to reflect our changing values when we deem it appropriate. We don't need a gang of white-collar criminals updating our Constitution for us. Our Constitution mandates that we enjoy a "Republican Form of Government," not an oligarchy of lawyers.

## STRICT SCRUTINY

In 1965 (*Griswold v. Connecticut*) the Supreme Court used the due process scam to nullify a Connecticut law prohibiting the use of birth control devices. The majority said the law

> "cannot stand in light of the familiar principle, so often applied by this Court, that a governmental purpose to control or prevent activities constitutionally subject to state regulation may not be achieved by means which sweep unnecessarily broadly and thereby invade the area of protected freedoms."

Justice Hugo Black, in a dissenting opinion, stated the obvious:

> "I do not believe that we are granted power by the Due Process Clause or any other constitutional provision or provisions to measure constitutionality by our belief that legislation is arbitrary, capricious or unreasonable, or accomplishes no justifiable purpose, or is offensive to our own notions of "civilized standards of conduct." Such an appraisal of the wisdom of legislation is an attribute of the power to make laws, not of the power to interpret them. The use by federal courts of such a formula or doctrine or whatnot to veto federal or state laws simply takes away from Congress and States the power to make laws based on their own judgement of fairness and wisdom and transfers that power to this Court for ultimate determination - a power which was specifically denied to federal courts by the convention that framed the Constitution" [8].

Justice Black did not continue and state what is equally obvious: his "brethren" who had the gall to usurp "veto" power over legislation because they thought it "arbitrary, capricious or unreasonable" were nothing but a bunch of white collar criminals. Black knew that much honesty would be an unseemly breach of judicial decorum.

Here's a summary of what the Supreme Court has twisted the "due process clause" in the Fifth and Fourteenth Amendments to mean:

Any exercise of "legislative Powers" is subject to the approval of the Supreme Court. The Court will veto any law that a favored plaintiff finds inconvenient and a majority of the Court's members think lacks a "rational basis." That is it does not "rationally relate to a legitimate governmental interest." The Court gets to determine what's "rational" and which governmental interests are "legitimate."

Even if it considers a law to be "rational" and the underlying governmental interests "legitimate" the Court will subject the law to "strict scrutiny" if it impinges on "fundamental rights." In such cases the justices will veto it unless they opine that it furthers a "compelling" governmental interest and is "narrowly drawn" to serve that interest. The "fundamental rights" don't have to be mentioned in the Constitution. If the justices want them to be "fundamental," they're "fundamental," even if they involve acts that were illegal when the Fifth and 14th Amendments were ratified [9].

As a practical matter, it seems that Congress might be able to override a judicial "veto" in any one of four ways. It could start the wheels in motion to "pack" the Court. The last time this was tried it motivated a justice to abandon his criminal ways.

The second method is the least desirable. With a two-thirds super-majority in both Houses and the support of three-fourths of the states, Congress can amend the Constitution to override the veto. But that action legitimizes the justices' criminal act. Besides, the Supreme

Court might then rule that Congress did not intend the new Amendment to mean what Congress thought it intended the Amendment to mean. That's how the Court perverted the 14th Amendment.

The third method is more desirable than the second, but just as difficult. Congress can impeach and remove a Supreme Court majority for usurpation of "legislative Powers," an offence that certainly qualifies as a "high crime." Then, after the miscreant justices are replaced, invite the Court to reconsider the usurpation. This approach would probably drive a stake into the heart of the due process scam. But its use would require a higher class of U. S. Senator than "We the People" are ever likely to have in our employ [10].

The fourth method is a lot easier than impeachment. Congress can rein in the federal courts by legislation. Language in the Constitution gives it the right to restrict the "appellate jurisdiction" of the Supreme Court. And it can pass a new "Judiciary Act," placing endless restrictions on judicial mischief at all levels. About the only thing it can't do is reduce or eliminate judicial salaries without impeaching and removing somebody.

### CHAPTER 4 END NOTES
1. See Connolly, 2010, Chapter 1.
2. Ibid., Chapter 4.
3. Hamilton's statement was made in a speech to the New York Assembly in Feb. 1787. To review the historical meaning of "due process," see Berger (Chapter 11), Crosskey (Vol. II, Chapter XXXII) and the book by Hugo Black. Hamilton's attitude towards judicial power is discussed in Bowers (1953). In a debate with Thomas Jefferson, Hamilton is reported to have said, "the people,

sir, is nothing but a great beast." See Platt (page 251).

4. Maryland's anti-blasphemy statute provided for a punishment of "death without benefit of clergy" on the third offense. Massachusetts law provided the death penalty for blasphemy, idolatry, and witchcraft. See Saunders, pages 90-95. See also Chapters XXXI and XXXII in Volume II of Crosskey.

5. Section 5 of the 14th Amendment says: "The Congress shall have power to enforce, by appropriate legislation, the provisions of this article." For the source of Lincoln's statement quoted above see the previous Chapter.

6. See Connolly, 2010, Chapters 12 and 13.

7. After a 52 word preamble, the first sentence in the Constitution is "All legislative Powers herein granted shall be vested in a Congress of the United States . . . "

8. One can confirm the truth of Justice Black's last statement by reviewing the record of debates at the Constitutional Convention. See Connolly, 2010, Chapter 8.

9. The phrases in quotation marks in the last two paragraphs can be found in numerous federal court opinions and countless lectures by constitutional law professors. To review their use in those contexts, pick any major Internet search engine you like and perform a search on the key words: "substantive due process," "strict scrutiny," and "rational basis."

10. The history of the substantive due process doctrine is also reviewed in the 1977 book by Professor Raoul Berger. Check the Bibliography.

# CHAPTER 5: TREASON HAS FOUND A REFUGE

If you owned a small business and you learned that your employees were stealing from you, what would you do? Let's review some of the fraudulent acts perpetrated by your judicial employees in the name of the "due process clause" of the 14th Amendment. Then you can decide what to do about it. Our judicial employees told us that the due process clause of the 14th Amendment protects flag burning. Yet our founders who adopted the 14th Amendment treated public desecration of the American flag as treason and punished it with death [1].

Our employees assert that the 'due process clause' forbids gender discrimination in all state and local programs. But other language within the 14th Amendment expressly permits, even encourages, gender discrimination by the states in federal elections [2].

Our employees claimed that the 14th Amendment mandates forced busing to integrate public schools. That would be a big surprise to the congressmen who framed it in 1866. They intended quite the opposite and they said so on the record. The Thirty Ninth Congress, which drafted the 14th Amendment, also passed legislation that retained racial segregation in the Washington, D.C. schools. When the Senate voted to adopt the 14th Amendment, it had separate black and white sections in its visitors' gallery [3].

The Supreme Court claims that the 14th Amendment forbids any meaningful state restrictions on abortion. Yet, when the states ratified the Amendment, most of them had anti abortion laws on the books. They passed or toughened many of those laws in the 1860's and 1870's, right around the same time they ratified the 14th Amendment. And Congress passed laws in 1865 and 1872 making it a criminal offense to send abortion information through the mail. Our judicial employees tell us that, at the same time Congress and the states were passing laws against abortion, they amended the Constitution to nullify all those laws [4].

Contemporaneous with the adoption of the 14th Amendment, Congress passed four "enforcement" acts, (in 1866, 1870, 1871, and 1875) as Section 5 of the Amendment expressly authorized. The text of those four acts, which ran in total to over 8000 words, was completely devoid of any language to support claims that the 14th Amendment protected flag burning or abortion, or demanded public school integration or gender equity in state programs [5].

It seems so obvious that our judicial employees are guilty of workplace fraud, you might wonder: How come they're not all in jail? Does anyone believe they're on the up and up?

The answers will depress you. Lots of people value the benefits of the workplace fraud more highly than they value the Constitution. So they support one or more of the three main cover stories slick lawyers have thought up to justify the fraud. Let's review those cover stories; somebody might try them on you. The first one goes something like this:

It's true that no one back then intended the 14th Amendment to protect flag burning or abortion. And no one intended it to demand gender equity or public school integration. But the Amendment's framers were very wise. They knew that we would need changes as time went on. So they used sweeping, vague language, guaranteeing things like "due process." They wanted to give the

Supreme Court the tools it needed to adapt the Constitution to the needs of changing times. Let's call this one the 'vague-on-purpose' story. The second cover story goes more or less as follows:

Prior to the ratification of the 14th Amendment, the Bill of Rights restricted only the federal government. But the framers of the 14th Amendment decided to change that. They intended the Amendment's 'due process clause' to incorporate the Bill of Rights against the states so that federal courts would be able to force the states to honor our basic civil rights. Let's call this one the "incorporation" cover story.

The third main cover story is the most brazen of the three. Our Constitution "evolves" to conform to US Supreme Court opinions. Let's call this one the "evolving Constitution" cover story. We'll put off discussing it until chapter 6.

A review of the history of the 14th Amendment reveals that all three cover stories are not only false, they're ridiculous. We'll take them one at a time.

## THE 'VAGUE-ON-PURPOSE' COVER STORY

There are, at least, four reasons to reject the "vague on purpose" cover story. The first reason involves language in the 14th Amendment itself. Its Section 5 explicitly assigns enforcement power to "Congress," not the courts. Congress included Section 5 in response to a recent Supreme Court power grab, the Dred Scott decision.

> "The Congress shall have power to enforce, by appropriate legislation, the provisions of this article."

That language wasn't used in Constitutional Amendments until after the Civil War. Congress then began including such language to preclude a repetition of judicial mischief like the Dred Scott Decision. The Court actually admitted that Section 5 was intended to reserve enforcement power to Congress for a decade or so after the 14th Amendment was passed. In 1879, in Ex Parte Virginia, our judicial employees wrote:

> "It is not said (in the 14th Amendment, that) the judicial power of the general government shall . . . be authorized to declare void any action of a State in violation of (its) prohibitions. It is the power of Congress which has been enlarged. Congress is authorized to enforce the prohibitions by appropriate legislation." [6]

The second reason is simple and obvious. The framers of the 14th Amendment obviously knew the proper way to adapt the Constitution to meet the needs of changing times. They did it three times within the space of five years, adopting the Thirteenth Amendment in 1865, the 14th in 1868, and the Fifteenth in 1870. They used the method that the Constitution expressly requires us to use for that purpose.

The third reason involves the legislation referred to above that Congress passed to enforce the 14th Amendment. That legislation, which ran in aggregate to 8149 words, was quite specific and detailed. Over the years, the Supreme Court found pretexts to nullify most of it because the justices found it distasteful. Nevertheless, it's beyond honest dispute that the enforcement legislation expressed the intent of our founders in framing and ratifying the 14th Amendment. The Congresses that passed the enforcement legislation were contemporaneous with and dominated by the same political party as the Congress that framed the 14th Amendment and most of the state legislatures that ratified it.

The fourth reason is the clincher. At the time the 14th Amendment was drafted and ratified, distrust for the Supreme Court was at an all-time high. According to a Lincoln biographer, the Republicans (who sponsored the 14th Amendment) viewed Chief Justice Taney's death in 1864 as "the removal of a barrier to human progress." In May 1861, the New York Tribune wrote that Chief Justice Taney "takes sides with traitors . . . throwing about them the sheltering protection of the ermine." That same year the New York Times observed that Chief Justice Taney would "go through history as the judge who dragged his official robes in the pollutions of treason." The Chicago Tribune called the Supreme Court "the last entrenchment behind which Despotism (sic) is sheltered." [7]

In December 1866, The Washington Chronicle wrote, "treason had found a refuge in the bosom of the Supreme Court of the United States." In March 1867, Harper's Weekly accused the Court of trying to "reverse the results of the war". In April 1867, the National Independent wrote that the Supreme Court was "regarded as a diseased member of the body politic," and was at risk of "amputation." Much of this criticism of the Court occurred while the 14th Amendment was before the states for ratification. [8]

Members of Congress who framed the 14th Amendment were also disgusted with the Court. They believed that it was usurping "political" power and that one of its usurpations had caused the Civil War. In January 1864, John P. Hale, of New Hampshire, made the following statement on the floor of the Senate [9].

> "I will take this occasion to say that in my humble judgement if there was a single, palpable, obvious

duty that the Republican party owed to themselves, owed to the country, owed to humanity, owed to God when they came into power, it was to drive a plowshare from turret to foundation stone of the Supreme Court "

In 1865, Congressman Thaddeus Stevens of Pennsylvania expressed the opinion that recently deceased Chief Justice Taney was "damned . . . to everlasting fire." Below are excerpts from a speech given in the House of Representatives by John A. Bingham, of Ohio. Bingham has been described by historians as "the leading House moderate" on the Joint Committee on Reconstruction (the committee which drafted the 14th Amendment). In January 1867, Bingham proposed "sweeping away at once the court's appellate jurisdiction in all cases." He went on to say,

"if, however, the Court usurps power to decide political questions and defy a free people's will, it will only remain for a people thus insulted and defied to demonstrate that the servant is not above his lord, by procuring a further Constitutional amendment and ratifying the same, which will defy judicial usurpation, by annihilating the usurper's (amendment) in the abolition of the tribunal itself."

That's pretty strong language for "the leading House moderate" among the 14th Amendment's framers. It underscores the degree of mistrust of the Supreme Court held by those framers [9].

In March 1868 Congress passed a law (The Judiciary Act of 1868) which reduced the scope of the Supreme Court's appellate jurisdiction. A little later, in *Ex Parte McCardle*, the Court unanimously upheld the law. The justices swallowed this bitter pill because the law had recently passed in the Senate by a vote of 33-9 and in the House by 115-57. Its sponsors probably had the votes to impeach and remove as many Supreme Court justices as they thought necessary [10].

This is not the sort of climate in which Congress would give the Court a blank check to revise the Constitution to meet the needs of changing times. In the 1860's, Congress viewed an out-of-control judiciary as the problem, not the solution.

## THE "INCORPORATION" COVER STORY

If the 14th Amendment empowered federal courts to enforce the Bill of Rights against the states, this was one of the best-kept secrets in American history. There was no clue to this intent in the four enforcement laws that Congress passed contemporaneous with the Amendment. Furthermore, the Supreme Court itself was totally unaware of this sweeping new power a scant nine months after the Amendment was ratified. The Court decided *Twitchell v. Pennsylvania* on April 5, 1869. Mr. Twitchell had been convicted of murder under a process that his lawyer claimed violated the Fifth and Sixth Amendments. The Supreme Court (unanimously) disposed of the case by citing the original understanding that the Bill of Rights restricted only the federal government, not the states. Nobody mentioned the 14th Amendment. If the 14th Amendment was intended to "incorporate" the Bill of Rights against the states, you would think that nine months after it was ratified somebody would have known about this intent, either the plaintiff's lawyer, or one of the nine eminent lawyers on the 1869 Supreme Court [11].

In 1876, Congress debated, and almost passed, a resolution to recommend to the states a proposed constitutional amendment to impose the First Amendment's religious freedom mandates on the states. The so-called "Blaine Amendment" said,

> "No State shall make any laws respecting an establishment of religion or prohibiting the free exercise thereof; and no money raised by taxation in any State for the support of public schools, or derived from any public fund therefor, nor any public lands devoted thereto, shall ever be under the control of any religious sect, nor shall any money so raised or lands so devoted be divided between religious sects or denominations."

Many of the folks who voted to adopt or ratify the 14th Amendment were (still) in Congress when it debated the Blaine Amendment. They surely remembered what they had done, and intended, a scant eight years earlier. They would not have bothered with a new Amendment to redo what they had already accomplished with the 14th [12].

A law professor named Stanley Morrison reviewed a dozen different cases between 1868 and 1947 in which various defense lawyers asserted that the Bill of Rights restricts the states as well as the federal government. For the first two decades the 14th Amendment wasn't even mentioned. It wasn't until 1887, nineteen years after the Amendment was added to the Constitution, that a resourceful lawyer decided to try the "incorporation" story line.

Charles Fairman, a colleague of Professor Morrison's, performed an exhaustive review of historical material which might illuminate the intent of the framers of the 14th Amendment with respect to the "incorporation" claim. He studied the debates in Congress, speeches by congressmen campaigning for reelection in 1866, proceedings in the various state legislatures that ratified the Amendment, and relevant articles in the major newspapers of the time. Then he wrote a lengthy article reporting what he found [13].

In summarizing, Professor Fairman wrote that he found a "mountain of evidence" debunking the incorporation story line and only a few "stones and pebbles" to support it. That probably explains why it took the Supreme Court a generation to learn about the story [13].

## THE "INCORPORATION" COVER STORY, PART 2

At the risk of being tedious, I'll present another reason why most of the folks who adopted the 14th Amendment couldn't possibly have intended its 'due process clause' to incorporate any or all of the Bill of Rights against the states. This argument is due to Andrew T. Hyman [14].

Those who framed the 14th Amendment and voted to propose and/or ratify it were not a bunch of idiots. They knew about the Fifth Amendment. And they undoubtedly intended the 'due process clause' in the 14th Amendment to mean whatever they understood the same language to mean in the Fifth Amendment. The Fifth Amendment was framed, proposed, and ratified at more or less the same time as the other nine Amendments in the Bill of Rights.

Our original Founders were not a bunch of idiots either. They would not have framed, proposed, and ratified ten Amendments if they intended one of them (the Fifth) to contain everything said in most of the other nine. The conclusion is inescapable: the 'due process clause' in the 14th Amendment was not intended to incorporate the Bill of Rights against the states.

You may think I've just implied that most of our supreme judicial employees for the last 130 years have been a bunch of idiots. That's not it at all. Is the mafia a bunch of idiots?

**CHAPTER 5 END NOTES**

1. See Chapter 23 of Connolly, 2010.

2. See Chapter 24 of Connolly, 2010. The 14th Amendment has five Sections. It can be found, along with the rest of the Constitution, in any encyclopedia or in Connolly's Appendix A.

3. See page 68 of the essay by Tribe in A Matter of Interpretation, by Antonin Scalia. An account of the 14th Amendment's history relative to school segregation can be found in Berger, 1977, Chapters 4 and 7.

4. See Mohr, 1978, pages 195-225 to review the history of mid 19th Century abortion laws.

5. At the time of this writing the four 14th Amendment Enforcement Acts could be found on the Internet at http://www.ttokarnak.net/14AEActs.html. They can also be found in Appendix B of Connolly 2010.

6. Professor Raoul Berger's historical review (see his Chapter 12) showed beyond honest doubt that the framers intended the language in Section 5 to withhold enforcement power from the courts. The quote from *Ex Parte Virginia* can be found in Berger on page 221.

7. See Silver, pages 223, 231, 232, and 239.

8. See Warren, Volume III, pages 170, 174, and 181. The 14th Amendment was adopted by Congress on June 13, 1866 and ratified by a sufficient number of states on July 9, 1868.

9. The quote attributed to Senator Hale can be found in Silver, page 139. The quote attributed to Congressman Stevens can be found in a footnote on page 222 of Berger, 1977. The description of John A. Bingham as "the leading House moderate" was on page 86 of Maltz. The Bingam

quote was taken from Warren, Volume III, pages 170-171. Most of the quote also appears in Boudin, Vol. II, page 75.

10. See Murphy, Walter F, page 27. See also Warren, Vol. Three, pages 195 - 210.

11. See Fairman, page 212, 213.

12. See http://en.wikipedia.org/wiki/Blaine_Amendment.

13. Check the Bibliography. Fairman's article is on pages 85-219 of Fairman and Morrison. A political scientist named Horace Flack published a book in 1908 in which he presented all the evidence he could find to support the "incorporation theory." The evidence was a bit scanty. And the few scraps there were only supported the claim that Congress intended Section 5 to empower itself to bring the States under the Bill of Rights, using the "privileges and immunities" clause, should it choose to do so. Flack found no evidence whatever which indicated that Congress intended the 14th Amendment's "due process clause" to empower the Supreme Court to "usurp power to decide political questions."

14. Mr. Hyman's analysis of the history of the due process clause can be found in the Akron Law Review (38 Akron Law Rev. 1 (2005)). It can also be found on the Internet at http://www.andrewhyman.com/due.html. As you've probably guessed, I've taken some liberties with Mr. Hyman's language.

# CHAPTER 6: OUR EVOLVING CONSTITUTION

Imagine that you live in Plum Creek, a fictitious, medium size town somewhere in the United States. It has two high schools; East High and West High. The rivalry between the two schools' football teams has been a major feature of local culture for decades. Last year, a boy living next door to your home was playing on the West High team. He invited you to attend the season finale, the game against East High. It began with the usual rules. However, East High couldn't seem to move the ball. The team had big, strong players; but they were slow and they had no passing game. The referees reacted by announcing some rule changes. From now on, a team only needed thirty-nine and one half inches for a first down. And it had five attempts rather than four, but only if it didn't try a pass play. Any forward pass would end a series of downs.

People sitting near you in the stands were quite upset about the changes. They knew that two of the three referees were uncles, and the third a next door neighbor, of East High players. A committee elected by all the high school coaches in the state had hired the referees. But they had long term contracts, and it was almost impossible to get rid of one who was biased, corrupt, or incompetent.

Many years ago, the coaches committee had also written a rule book; and all the coaches had then voted to adopt it. It said that no rule could be changed without the written approval of three-fourths of the coaches. It also said, "A first down requires an advance of ten yards or more in no more than four plays." And it didn't say anything about special limits on pass plays. When irate fans complained

47

about the rule changes, the referees brushed them off. "You don't understand the rule book," they said, "it's a living document which evolves to meet the needs of changing times."

## A LIVING CONSTITUTION

Every so often the Supreme Court issues an opinion which proclaims some surprising new constitutional principle. Journalists then seek out law professors to explain why the strange new principle is really on the up and up. The law professors respond with complex and windy theories asserting that the principle is not new at all, it's just that nobody ever noticed it before. Never mind that it defies the plain language of the Constitution. Never mind that it also defies the well-documented intent of "We the People" at the time we allowed the relevant constitutional passages to be ratified. The law professors respond more or less along the following lines:

> 'Surely you don't want to be ruled by the ideas of people who've been dead for 200 years. Our founders knew that new problems would call for new solutions. So they gave us a living Constitution which would evolve to meet the needs of changing times.'

Then, in their spare time, they write books full of hokum to explain how fraudulent Supreme Court opinions are parts of the "living Constitution." And they teach the hokum to their students, the next generation of judges.

It seems quite likely that every law professor has read the Constitution at least once. So they all know about Article V which our founders included to provide a mechanism we could use to amend it, from time to time. Article V was included so we wouldn't have to choose

48

between being ruled by crooked employees and being ruled by the ideas of people who've been dead for 200 years.

## THE THEORY OF EVOLUTION

Let's all agree that it's nice to have a "living Constitution" which "evolves" to meet the needs of changing times. We've learned about two mechanisms of evolution; the one that is mandated by the Constitution itself, and the one that was made up by our judicial employees. In this section we'll explore which one is evolution and which one is grand larceny.

Darwin's theory of evolution depends on two key ideas, "random mutations" and "natural selection." Mutations are genetic accidents. The theory of evolution holds that they occur randomly, that is purely by chance. "Natural selection" is just another way of saying the survival of the fittest. The environment selects for survival those mutations best suited to survive and thrive in it. After many generations, descendants of the more "fit" mutants exist in great numbers and the less "fit" members of their ancestral species have died out. Operating over very long times, these processes can, according to Darwin's theory, bring about dramatic changes. For example, life scientists have claimed that modern birds evolved from dinosaurs [1].

The theory of evolution may be an apt metaphor to describe the legitimate (Article V) approach to evolving our Constitution. In a large, diverse republic numerous ideas for policy reform occur randomly each year. Most of them are not good (or popular) enough to justify amending our fundamental law. Occasionally the 'environment' (a consensus of "We the People" which persists for years) selects a new idea to include in the Constitution, displacing some old ideas in the process. It's happened twenty-seven

49

times since the dawn of the Republic.

On the other hand, the process by which judges "evolve" our Constitution is not at all consistent with the theory of "evolution." Mutants born in the Supreme Court do not have to survive any meaningful test of fitness. A special interest group conceives a scheme to amend our Constitution without obtaining the consent of "We the People." Its lawyers take the scheme to the U. S. Supreme Court. A majority of the nine lawyer-politicians on the Court like the scheme. It serves their personal biases. Or it tends to increase their power. So they hand down a decision that defies the plain meaning of the constitutional language they invoke to support it. Fit or unfit, the principle of stare decisis nurtures and protects all the mutants produced thereby. This kind of evolution kills off perfectly good members of our living Constitution and replaces them with a menagerie of freaks. Songbirds disappear and are replaced by mean, ugly dinosaurs.

## CHAPTER 6 END NOTES

1. See, for example, "Feathered Dinosaur Ruffles Paleontology," USN&WR, July 6, 1998, page 62, an article by Laura Tangley. This claim is disputed by other scientists. Our description of the theory of evolution is from the National Academy publication by Kennedy and others. See the Bibliography.

# CHAPTER 7: EDICTS OF THE "SECULAR PAPACY"

In 1791, when our founders adopted the First Amendment, ten of the thirteen states had officially established religions. They intended the First Amendment to protect state and local autonomy in religious matters from federal interference. That's why it begins, "Congress shall make no law . . ." It never occurred to our founders that the Supreme Court might gradually usurp Congress's most important law making powers.

The fact that the founders intended the First Amendment to restrict only the federal government is beyond dispute. The Marshall Court admitted it (unanimously) in 1833. The name of the case was *Barron v. Baltimore.* In 1833, the justices knew that the truth about the origins of the Bill-of-Rights was still fresh in our collective memory. The kind of deceptions our judicial employees get away with now would have been political suicide back then.

Around 1940, about 150 years after we adopted the First Amendment and 70 years after we adopted the 14th, the Supreme Court started using the due process scam to create a bogus new First Amendment out of whole cloth. The Court asserted that the due process clause of the 14th Amendment made states, cities, towns, villages, and public schools subject to the Bill of Rights. The justices also claimed that the due process clause empowered the Court to "evolve" the Bill of Rights, from time to time, so it would better conform to the judicial notions about "fundamental law" .

That claim was at best preposterous and at worst comical. When the 14th Amendment was adopted, shortly after the Civil War, the public and the Congress viewed the Supreme Court with great distrust. In designing the Amendment, its framers took pains to avoid trusting the Court with power to enforce it; they didn't want to rely on an institution then viewed as "a diseased member of the body politic." So they included Section 5 which explicitly assigned enforcement power to "Congress."

Contemporaneous with the adoption of the 14th Amendment, Congress passed four Enforcement Acts as the Amendment's Section 5 expressly authorized and implicitly promised. There was not a word about religion; there was not a word about separation of church and state; there was not a word about incorporating the First Amendment or any part of the Bill of Rights against the states. There was not even a hint about authorizing our judicial employees to invent a mountain of new content in our centuries-old right to "due process of law." So the Supreme Court's claimed power to enforce its lobotomy on the First Amendment against the States is, to put it kindly, without foundation [1].

To put it more plainly, the claim is a brazen fraud. In 1876, a scant eight years after the 14th Amendment was ratified, Congress debated another proposed amendment to impose the substance of the First Amendment on the states. The proposed "Blaine Amendment" had a fair amount of support. It passed in the House with 180 yeas, 7 nays, and 98 not voting. It failed in the Senate with 28 yeas, 16 nays, and 27 not voting. In roughly the same time frame, many of the states placed similar language in their own constitutions. So it's clear that the idea of imposing First Amendment principles on the states was popular at the time. But it wasn't quite popular enough to support amending the U. S. Constitution. It's also clear that the

14th Amendment was not intended to "incorporate" the First Amendment against the states. Many of the Congressmen who voted to adopt the 14th Amendment were still around in 1876 to debate and vote on the Blaine Amendment. They would certainly remember what they had done, and intended, eight years earlier [2].

## SNEAKING LIKE A THIEF, OVER THE FIELD OF JURISDICTION

In the majority opinion in *Everson v. Board of Education* (1947), Justice Hugo Black, a former member of the Ku Klux Klan, wrote,

> "In the words of Jefferson, the clause against establishment of religion by law was intended to erect "a wall of separation between church and State."

Thomas Jefferson's statement misrepresented by Justice Black, had nothing to do with the 14th Amendment. The statement was included in a letter to the Danbury Baptist Association, which was written in 1802. When the 14th Amendment, which our unfaithful judicial employees claim "incorporated" the First Amendment against the states, was adopted Jefferson was long dead.

If everything ever written by Thomas Jefferson is to be taken as part of the Constitution, how about the following passage from his 1821 letter to Charles Hammond: [3]

> "(The) federal judiciary (is) an irresponsible body (for impeachment is scarcely a scarecrow) working like gravity by night and by day, gaining a little today and little tomorrow, and advancing its noiseless step like a thief, over the field of jurisdiction . . ."

Our "federal judiciary" has been "advancing it noiseless

53

step like a thief, over the field of jurisdiction" for two centuries. It has usurped the most important "legislative Powers" our founders assigned to "Congress." That is a crime against the Constitution and the American people. The American people, unfortunately, have no good way to prevent or punish this crime. Throughout our history, Congress has showed itself unwilling, or unable, to defend the Constitution against a renegade Court.

## OUR SECULAR RELIGION

Now it's time to share another dirty little secret. Federal courts have not only trashed the First Amendment by restricting our free exercise of religion, they've also trashed it by establishing an official federal government religion. Legal scholars and historians have been bragging about this for more than a century. The substance of their boasts can be summarized more or less as follows. America's dominant religion is now a "secular religion." The bogus constitution that the Court made up over the years is its bible. The real Constitution, the one that begins "We the People," has been degraded to the status of an empty symbol. It fills the need of the unsophisticated masses to venerate something. Lawyers and judges are the secular religion's priests and Supreme Court justices are its high priests [4].

Law professor A. S. Miller, for example, refers to the Supreme Court Building as "The Temple on the Hill" and the Court itself as a "theological institution." He characterizes as "sacred documents" the bogus constitution that the Court made up. Miller refers to the justices as "High Priests," and points out that the "Court cannot be understood apart from its religious aspects" [5].

Professor Miller also quotes fellow legal scholars who

assert that the justices are "brushed with divinity," and refer to lawyers as a "priestly tribe" which defends "this Arc of the Covenant (the bogus constitution)" against the "profane touch" of "open and covert foes" (presumably "We the People") [6].

Constitutional law literature is loaded with such quotes; Miller's book is only one of the richer sources. In 1880 Oliver Wendell Holmes, a legal deep thinker of the time, wrote an article in which he referred to the Dean of Harvard Law school as "the greatest living legal theologian." Friends of the Supreme Court have called it the "secular papacy" [7].

## AN ECCLESIASTICAL PRINCIPALITY

The actions of our Supreme Court can usually be understood by studying Niccolo Machiavelli's The Prince. One lesson it taught stood out from all the others. That lesson concerned the most reliable way for a "Prince" to secure his power. He should establish and maintain an "Ecclesiastical Principality." He should set up a state in which the ruler enjoys the protection of an official religion.

In medieval England, the birthplace of America's legal tradition, the rulers understood Machiavelli's lessons even before he did. English kings ruled by "divine right." They were the anointed of God. If you didn't obey them you were going to hell. You were going to hell after they cut off your head, of course [8].

English common law judges were agents of the king. So they also claimed to speak for God. This was a basic part of their act. They took on the trappings of priests. They dressed in robes, practiced rituals, and did business in Latin. Judges in England's American colonies followed suit. After America became independent, our Supreme

Court still claimed to speak for God's law; it just didn't mention God.  It justified constitutionally unfounded decisions by reference to "natural law" or "fundamental law."  The justices claimed that they spoke for law that was "sacred" or law that existed before the Constitution and even before "society" [9].

The "secular papacy" now tries to avoid making its game so obvious.  The justices don't say that God comes down to give them instructions at 3:00 every Tuesday afternoon.  They also never say, "listen up, this is your god speaking."  That would be much too clumsy.  Instead they say that they have "discovered" what "fundamental law" says about the issue in question.

Once in a while the Court slips up and blows its cover.  During the Vietnam War years, it laid down rules for use in deciding what is, or isn't, a religion.  Congress had passed a law that allowed conscientious objectors to avoid serving in the military.   The law said that those who believed that all war was sinful didn't have to serve.  But the basis of their belief had to be a religion.  The law in question exempted from

> "combatant service in the armed forces those who are conscientiously opposed to participation in war by reason of their "religious training and belief," i.e., belief in an individual's relation to a Supreme Being involving duties beyond a human relationship but not essentially political, sociological, or philosophical views or a merely personal moral code" [10].

Some men who admitted that they did not believe in God demanded to escape the draft under those laws anyway.  The draft boards didn't buy it.  So the men sued in federal court.  They said that a federal draft exemption based on "religion" violated the First Amendment, an entirely reasonable claim.

Several cases got to the Supreme Court which, at that time, was even more liberal than it is now. The justices, therefore, wanted to find a way to let the draft dodgers off the hook. However, if they accepted the obvious truth that the law violated the First Amendment, nobody would be able to use it to escape military service. That was not the policy outcome they wanted. So they resorted to the ludicrous claim that the law did not violate the First Amendment. But it embodied an amazing new meaning for the word, "religion." Never mind that "Supreme Being" stuff.

Our judicial employees said that a "religion" did not necessarily include belief in God, or prayer, or any of the usual things. In 1965, in *Seeger v. United States*, the Court ruled that a religion was any "sincere and meaningful belief occupying in the life of its possessor a place parallel to that filled by the God of those admittedly qualifying for the (draft) exemption [10]."

It gets even better. In 1970, in *Welsh v. United States*, the Court opined that you could have a religion without even calling it a religion. On that occasion your judicial employees said:

> "In view of the broad scope of the word 'religious,' a registrant's characterization of his beliefs as 'nonreligious' is not a reliable guide to those administering the (draft) exemption [11]."

It's beyond honest doubt that the definition of "religion" given in those two opinions was not the one intended by the congressmen who wrote and voted for the Act. So the opinions were fraudulent. However, that definition is really quite close to the thinking of academic experts on religion.

Experts say, for example, that a religion is any "total commitment to an all-embracing group goal . . . an ultimate concern" [12].

OK. Let's go with that. What does a typical Supreme Court justice view as "an ultimate concern"? What are his most "sincere and meaningful" beliefs? His most sincere and meaningful beliefs include the sacred status of judicial power. They include the doctrine of stare decisis. They include the contents of the bogus constitution that they made up over the years. Federal courts have long imposed those doctrines on all Americans while restricting our free practice of religions that compete with theirs.

## THE TWO GREAT COMMANDMENTS OF ACLUISM

In defiance of the First Amendment, our judicial branch of government has been running a religious institution since colonial times. However, the tenets of that religion don't remain the same; they evolve over time in keeping with the religious bias of the Court majority. That's what law professors mean when they tell us that the Constitution "evolves."

For the last half-century or so, the Court's religion has embodied the doctrines of the American Civil Liberties Union (ACLU), a religious organization if ever there was one. Since it can't admit that the justices are fronting for a perverse and Godless religion, the ACLU doesn't call its sect by a religious name, i. e. one that ends in "ism." However, a thoughtful observer can easily see through the deception. The "secular religion" currently imposed on you by your judicial employees should be called "Acluism."

The central ideas of Acluism can be summarized by two great commandments. They have nothing in common with

58

the two Great Commandments revealed to followers of Christ in Matthew, Chapter 22. And they're never disclosed publicly by disciples of the ACLU. But they can be discovered by a careful study of the ideas the ACLU sells to the federal courts.

I. If there's a God, he'd better not show his face around here.

II. You must punish the innocent and reward the guilty.

**CHAPTER 7 END NOTES**

1. At the time of this writing the four 14th Amendment Enforcement Acts could be found on the Internet at http://www.ttokarnak.net/14AEActs.html. They can also be found in Appendix B of Connolly 2010.

2. A transcript of the proposed federal Blaine Amendment can be found on the Internet.

3. A transcript of Jefferson's letter to the Danbury Baptist association can be found at http://candst.tripod.com/tnppage/danbury.htm. A transcript of his 1821 letter to Charles Hammond can be found at http://www.barefootsworld.net/tjletters.html#hammond1821. And a facsimile of the Hammond letter can be found at a Library of Congress web site, http://memory.loc.gov/service/mss/mtj/mtj1/052/0900/0950.gif.

4. See, for example, Levinson (1988), who cites many earlier works on the subject. See also Miller (Arthur S., 1982).

5. See Miller (A. S. 1982), pages 1, 10, 19, and 20.

6. See Miller (A. S. 1982), pages 20 and 78.

7. The Oliver Wendell Holmes quote is from Glendon, 1994, page 186. Daniel Boorstin used the term "secular papacy" in the forward to Professor McCloskey's famous

book, The American Supreme Court.

8. Machiavelli wrote **The Prince** about the time of Shakespeare.

9. These quotes were taken from Konefsky, pages 131 and 142. Konefsky attributes the first ("most sacred" legal principles) to a biography of Marshall by Justice Joseph Story. He attributes the second (laws that existed before society) to the majority opinion in *Sturges v. Crowninshield,* (1819).

10. This passage is quoted from the Supreme Court opinion in *Seeger v. United States*.

11. See the majority opinion in *Welsh v. United States.*

12. The academic definition of religion is from Noss (1980, page 173). Noss was quoting Paul Tillich.

# BIBLIOGRAPHY

Abbott, Richard H; *The Republican Party and the South*, The University of North Carolina Press, 1986.

Acheson, Patricia; *The Supreme Court: America's Judicial Heritage*, Dodd Mead, 1961.

Behe, Michael J.; *Darwin's Black Box*, The Free Press, 1996.

Berger, Raoul; *Government by Judiciary: The Transformation of the Fourteenth Amendment*, Harvard U. Press, 1977.

Black, Hugo; *A Constitutional Faith*, Alfred A. Knopf, 1968.

Bork, Robert H.; *The Tempting of America: The Political Seduction of the Law*; A Touchstone Book, Simon & Schuster, 1990.

Boudin, Louis B.; *Government by Judiciary, Volume I and II*, William Godwin Inc., 1932

Bowers, Claude G.; *Jefferson and Hamilton*, Houghton Mifflin, 1953.

Connolly, D. J.; *The Temple of Karnak: How Rogue Judges Have Been Strangling Your Democracy*, Plum Creek Book Works, Jan. 2000

Connolly, D. J.: *Grand Larceny: An Unexpurgated History of the Supreme Court*; Amazon.com Create Space; 2010

Crosskey, William Winslow; *Politics and the Constitution in the History of the United States*, Volumes I and II, U. Chicago Press, 1953.

Crosskey, William Winslow. and Jeffrey, William Jr.; *Politics and the Constitution in the History of the United States, Volume III*, U. Chicago Press, 1980.

61

D'Souza, Dinesh; *The End of Racism*, The Free Press, 1995.

Fairman, Charles; *History of the Supreme Court of the United States, Vol. VI, Part I, "Reconstruction and Reunion, 1864-88"*; Macmillan Co.; 1971.

Fairman, Charles and Morrison, Stanley; *The Fourteenth Amendment and the Bill of Rights: The Incorporation Theory*, DeCapo Press, New York, 1970. This work contains reprints of articles, by the respective authors, which appeared in the December 1949 issue of the Stanford Law Review.

Fehrenbacher, Don. E.; *The Dred Scott Case: Its Significance in American Law and Politics*, Oxford U. Press, 1978.

Flack, Horace E.; *The Adoption of the Fourteenth Amendment*, Johns Hopkins University Press, 1908. Republished by Peter Smith, Gloucester, Mass., 1965.

Glendon, Mary Ann; *Abortion and Divorce in Western Law*, Harvard University Press, 1987.

Glendon, Mary Ann; *A Nation Under Lawyers*, Farrar, Giroux, 1994.

Grimes, Alan P.; *Democracy and the Amendments to the Constitution*, Lexington books, D. C. Heath and Co., 1978.

Heckman, Richard Allen; *Lincoln vs Douglas: The Great Debates Campaign*, Public Affairs Press, 1967.

Johnson, Phillip E.; *Darwin on Trial*, InterVarsity Press, 1993

Kennedy, Donald, National Academy Working Group Chairman, and others; *Teaching About Evolution*

*And the Nature of Science.* National Academy Press, Washington, DC, 1998.

Konefsky, Samuel J.; John Marshall and Alexander Hamilton - Architects of the American Constitution, The Macmillan Co., 1964.

Levinson, Sanford G.; *Constitutional Faith*, Princeton University Press, 1988.

Levinson, Sanford G.; *Preface to Second Edition and Added Chapters Eight and Nine in McCloskey, 1994.*

Levy, Leonard W.; *The Establishment Clause: Religion and the First Amendment*, MacMillan Publishing Co., 1986.

Licht, Robert A. et. al.; *The Framers and Fundamental Rights*, The AEI Press, American Enterprise Institute, 1992.

Lusky, Louis; *By What Right,* The Michie Company, Law Publishers, 1975

Machiavelli, Niccolo; *The Prince, With an Introduction by Henry Morley,* Third Edition, George Routledge and Sons, 1889.

Maltz, Earl M.; *Civil Rights, the Constitution, and Congress, 1863-1869,* University Press of Kansas, 1990.

McCloskey, Robert G.; *The American Supreme Court, Second Edition* , Revised by Sanford Levinson, University of Chicago Press, 1994.

McKeever, Robert J.; *Raw Judicial Power? The Supreme Court and American Society*, Manchester U. Press, U. S. Distribution by St. Martin's Press, 1993.

Miller, Arthur S.; *Toward Increased Judicial Activism: The Political Role of the Supreme Court*, Greenwood Press, 1982.

Mohr, James C.; *Abortion in America,* Oxford University Press, 1978.

Morrison, Stanley and Fairman, Charles; *The Fourteenth Amendment and the Bill of Rights: The Incorporation Theory*, DeCapo Press, New York, 1970. This work contains reprints of separate articles, by the respective authors, which appeared in the December 1949 issue of the Stanford Law Review.

Murphy,Walter F.; *Elements of Judicial Strategy*, U. of Chicago Press, 1964.

Noss, John B.; *Man's Religions*, Macmillan, 1980.

Phillips, Kevin; *The Cousins' Wars: Religion, Politics, & The Triumph Of Anglo-America,* Basic Books, 1999.

Platt, Suzy Ed.: *Respectfully Quoted: A Dictionary of Quotations Requested From the Congressional Research Service;* Library of Congress; 1989.

Price, William H.; *The Civil War Handbook*, L. B. Prince Company, Fairfax VA, 1961.

Rodell, Fred; *Woe Unto You Lawyers*, Pageant Press, 1957.

Saunders, Kevin W.; *Violence As Obscenity: Limiting the Media's First Amendment Protection*, Duke University Press, 1996.

Scalia, Antonin; *A Matter of Interpretation: Federal Courts and the Law*, Princeton U. Press, 1997. The book contains an essay by Justice Scalia and a Preface by Amy Gutman, Editor; as well as commentary by Gordon S. Wood, Laurence H. Tribe, Mary Ann Glendon, and Ronald Dworkin. It concludes with a response, to the commentary, by Scalia.

Silver, David M.; ***Lincoln's Supreme Court***, University of
    Illinois Press, 1998.

Swisher, Carl Brent; ***Roger B. Taney***, Macmillan, 1935.

Warren, Charles; ***The Supreme Court in United States
    History, Volumes I, II, and III*** .  Little Brown and
    Company, 1922.

Wells, Jonathan; ***Icons of Evolution: Science or Myth***,
    Regnery Publishing, 2000.

Woodward, Bob and Scott Armstrong; ***The Brethren:
    Inside the Supreme Court***, Avon Books, 1979.

www.ingramcontent.com/pod-product-compliance
Lightning Source LLC
Chambersburg PA
CBHW070836310526
45788CB00017B/1464